GEO

Question Mark

Mary Elizabeth Salzmann

Published by SandCastle™, an imprint of ABDO Publishing Company, 4940 Viking Drive, Edina, Minnesota 55435.

Printed in the United States.

Photo credits: PhotoDisc

Library of Congress Cataloging-in-Publication Data

Salzmann, Mary Elizabeth, 1968-
    Question mark / Mary Elizabeth Salzmann.
        p. cm. -- (Punctuation)
    Includes index.
    ISBN 1-57765-623-7
    1. English language--Punctuation--Juvenile literature. 2. English language--Interrogative--Juvenile literature. [1. English language--Punctuation. 2. English language--Interrogative.] I. Title.

PE1450 .S266 2001
428.2--dc21

2001033022

The SandCastle concept, content, and reading method have been reviewed and approved by a national advisory board including literacy specialists, librarians, elementary school teachers, early childhood education professionals, and parents.

Let Us Know

After reading the book, SandCastle would like you to tell us your stories about reading. What is your favorite page? Was there something hard that you needed help with? Share the ups and downs of learning to read. We want to hear from you! To get posted on the ABDO Publishing Company Web site, send us email at:

sandcastle@abdopub.com

About SandCastle™

Nonfiction books for the beginning reader

- Basic concepts of phonics are incorporated with integrated language methods of reading instruction. Most words are short, and phrases, letter sounds, and word sounds are repeated.

- Readability is determined by the number of words in each sentence, the number of characters in each word, and word lists based on curriculum frameworks.

- Full-color photography reinforces word meanings and concepts.

- "Words I Can Read" list at the end of each book teaches basic elements of grammar, helps the reader recognize the words in the text, and builds vocabulary.

- Reading levels are indicated by the number of flags on the castle.

Look for more SandCastle books
in these three reading levels:

Level 1 (one flag)	**Level 2** (two flags)	**Level 3** (three flags)

Grades Pre-K to K 5 or fewer words per page	**Grades K to 1** 5 to 10 words per page	**Grades 1 to 2** 10 to 15 words per page

This is a **question mark**.

I know when to use **question marks**.

Question marks end sentences that ask about something.

What is Rosa doing?

Emily is talented at playing music.

What instrument is she playing?

Cindy is grinning.

Why is she pointing to her mouth?

Jane and Victor are having a snack.

What kind of fruit are they eating?

Ken has a bunch of fall leaves.

What is he wearing to protect his hands?

What does Devon always wear when she rides her bicycle?

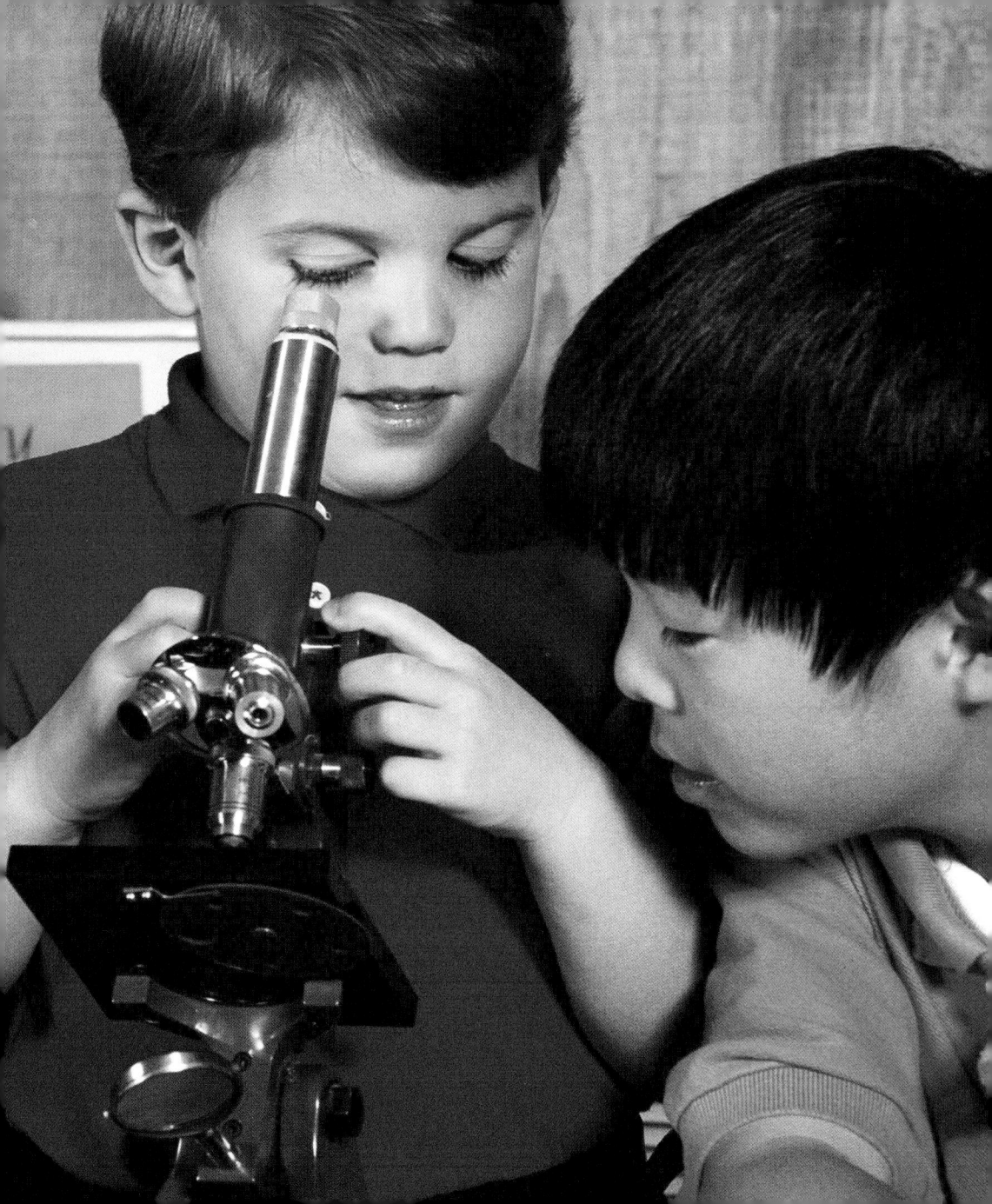

Frank and George are working on a science project.

What are they using?

Iris and Kendra are in the neighborhood pool.

What are they floating on?

(inner tubes)

Words I Can Read

Nouns

A noun is a person, place, or thing

bicycle (BYE-si-kuhl) p. 17
bunch (BUHNCH) p. 15
fall leaves (FAWL LEEVZ) p. 15
fruit (FROOT) p. 13
hands (HANDZ) p. 15
inner tubes (IN-ur toobz) p. 21
instrument (IN-struh-muhnt) p. 9

kind (KINDE) p. 13
mouth (MOUTH) p. 11
music (MYOO-zik) p. 9
neighborhood pool (NAY-bur-hud POOL) p. 21
question mark (KWESS-chuhn MARK) p. 5

question marks (KWESS-chuhn MARKSS) pp. 5, 7
science project (SYE-uhnss PROJ-ekt) p. 19
sentences (SEN-tuhnss-iz) p. 7
snack (SNAK) p. 13

Proper Nouns

A proper noun is the name of a person, place, or thing

Cindy (SIN-dee) p. 11
Devon (DEV-uhn) p. 17
Emily (EM-uh-lee) p. 9
Frank (FRANGK) p. 19

George (jorj) p. 19
Iris (EYE-riss) p. 21
Jane (JAYN) p. 13
Ken (KEN) p. 15

Kendra (KEN-druh) p. 21
Rosa (RO-zuh) p. 7
Victor (VIK-tur) p. 13

Pronouns

A pronoun is a word that replaces a noun

he (HEE) p. 15
I (EYE) p. 5
she (SHEE) pp. 9, 11, 17

something (SUHM-thing) p. 7
that (THAT) p. 7

they (THAY) pp. 13, 19, 21
this (THISS) p. 5
what (WUHT) pp. 7, 9, 13, 15, 17, 19, 21

Verbs

A verb is an action or being word

are (AR) pp. 13, 19, 21

ask (ASK) p. 7

does (DUHZ) p. 17

doing (DOO-ing) p. 7

eating (EET-ing) p. 13

end (END) p. 7

floating (FLOHT-ing) p. 21

grinning (GRIN-ing) p. 11

has (HAZ) p. 15

having (HAV-ing) p. 13

is (IZ) pp. 5, 7, 9, 11, 15

know (NOH) p. 5

playing (PLAY-ing) p. 9

pointing (POINT-ing) p. 11

protect (pruh-TEKT) p. 15

rides (RIDEZ) p. 17

use (YOOZ) p. 5

using (YOOZ-ing) p. 19

wear (WAIR) p. 17

wearing (WAIR-ing) p. 15

working (WURK-ing) p. 19

Adjectives

An adjective describes something

her (HUR) pp. 11, 17

his (HIZ) p. 15

talented (TAL-uhnt-ed) p. 9

Adverbs

An adverb tells how, when, or where something happens

always (AWL-waze) p. 17   **why** (WYE) p. 11

Glossary

bicycle – a vehicle with two wheels, a seat, handlebars to steer with, and pedals that you push with your feet

bunch – a group of things or people

fruit – the juicy part of a plant that you can eat and has one or more seeds

inner tubes – hollow rubber rings inside tires that are filled with air

instrument – something used to make music

neighborhood pool – a public swimming pool that is near where you live

snack – food you eat between meals